AN OCEAN OF DREAMS

FORTY-THREE POEMS

AN OCEAN OF DREAMS

FORTY-THREE POEMS

Mona Saudi

Translated by Tanya Tamari Nasir

Forward by David Malouf

PASSEGGIATA PRESS
Pueblo Colorado

© Mona Saudi

First English Language Edition
By Passeggiata Press 1999

Sa'udi, Muna.
[Muhit al-hulm.   English &Arabic]
An ocean of dreams :   forty-three poems / Mona Saudi : translated
by Tania Tamari Nasir ; foreword by David Malouf. -- 1st English
language ed.
p.   cm.
ISBN 1-57889-096-9
I. Nasir, Tania Tamari.   II.   Title
PJ7862.A78M8413   1999   99--13942
892.71'6--dc21   CIP

Photos of sculptures by Mona Saudi © by M. Saudi

"Mother Earth" Limestone, 1965

Foreword

Selected from thirty years' work, almost half a lifetime, these
forty and more poems are like Mona Saudi's sculptures, fragments
of a larger nature honed and given a shape that, in being so spare
and memorable, retain something of the larger entity, lived life in
this case rather than the geological stuff of landscape, from which
they have been cut; something too of the space that surrounds
them and the air and weather they once breathed. Once to silence
and the world of spirit, they are at the same time grounded in life
as it is lived in the body, and, since Mona Saudi is so acutely aware
of these things, of the body politic — and increasingly so as she
finds herself overtaken, as we all are, by 'history'. Her poems are
refershingly direct in statement yet manage to include much that
is just beyond expression; they have presence but speak eloquently
for what is absent, what has been lost or has not yet come into
being; she knows moments of anger and regret but what she cre-
ates in the end are acts of reconciliation, of a hard-won but deli-
cate resolution.

Those of us who do not know Arabic must be grateful for Tania
Tamari Nasir's fine translations, which are so precise, so rhyth-
mically varied and assured that they find a real voice in the new
language. They are firmly settled and at home there but have a
breath still of the other world they have come from, like the po-
ems themselves; migrating birds,to pick up one of Mona Saudi's
images, that have travelled across silence and distance to bring us
news of the joys and sorrows of being in the midst of life, of the
way chaos becomes order, of the self in joyful desolation, of the
'eternity', as Mona Saudi writes, 'of the visible',of natural objects
as 'the soul of the earth', of poems as attempts to recreate in words
'the silence of the stone'.

David Malouf

"A Woman With Wings" Marble, 1975

Contents

* Has Arabic original text on facing page

"Geometry of the Spirit" 1987,   Marble: 3 meters high
Set in front of the Institute of the Arab World, Paris

Preface

It all started over a year ago, when my friend Mona Saudi, a well known Jordanian sculptor asked if I might consider translating some of her Arabic poems into English. Mona was following up on a suggestion by the American poet, Jean Nordhaus, whom she had met earlier in Washington. Jean had thought that if Mona's poems were to be translated into English, they would find responsive readership in the West.

Mona knew I am not a professional writer or translator but she also knew of my appreciation of Arabic and English literature, as well as my admiration for her sculpture and her poetry. Although I have never done this kind of work before, I was excited by the challenge. At the same time, I was aware of the responsibility of translating a literary work - specially poetry, for I perceive poetry as the essence of self expression. Whether one writes it, reads it, translates it or listens to it, poetry is a pure declaration of the passions and of the intellect; a sacred exposure of the self, of private meaning, breathed out in moments of utter pain or ecstasy - to relieve the soul and to find solace in the written word. It is within this perception that I approached the task of translating Mona Saudi's poems and thus started a beautiful literary adventure: battling with words, meanings, ideas, but most of all battling with being true to the character and nature of the poems themselves.

I was fortunate to have Mona around for constant consultation. Together we selected the poems to be translated and we went over several "final" drafts. Each review led to more changes and alterations. When at moments I would find myself entangled in a complex web of poetic expression, I would turn to the ever indulgent Mona for help. As the mysteries unfolded, the Arabic poem would then gradually and smoothly transform itself and go on its English course.

Mona has written extensively and has published two volumes of poetry, *First Vision* (1972), and *An Ocean of Dreams* (1992). Although primarily known as a sculptor, Mona finds herself as easily in words as in stone. Of this special talent, Jabra Ibrahim Jabra, the prominent Arab writer and critic, wrote in his introduction to Mona's second book of poetry: "with Mona Saudi we enter unique vistas of creativity in the Arabic language, the like of which we cannot find for sheer excitement and vitality in any other Arab artist and which we can only find amongst a small group of artists in the West. For we know of painters and of sculptors who have written poetry and prose of a literary quality, but few are those who have been able to write creatively, totally independent of their primary art work: Mona Saudi belongs to this minority where the vision of the eye is entwined with the vision of the word, and where the one is constantly charged by the other."

When asked about her life and how she became an artist, Mona responded in an autobiographical article which she wrote in 1994 for a local Jordanian magazine. I quote parts of it here in translation as it bears personal witness to important milestones in her life and might enrich the reading and understanding of her poetry:

"I am constantly asked how did I become a sculptor. Shall I say that man begins with a dream in childhood ... I was born in 1945 in the city of Amman, Jordan, and Amman at that time was a small town, growing around water springs, old archaeological sites and rocky hills where natural caves housed local shepherds. Our house was at the entrance to a Roman nymphaeum, where I lived with my large extended family that originally came from Damascus, Syria, and settled in Amman at the end of the last century. About a hundred meters away were the ruins of a Roman amphitheater, and my childhood playgrounds were the ancient sprawling steps, the chiseled columns with their decorated capitals, the scattered fragments of statues and figures. I used to leave my friends and run to play with the statues, trying to find how is it that life can be infused in stone. For these statues were alive for me and these places, real and imaginary, made me realize that man is capable of producing great immortal works ...

"I was ten years old when Fathi, one of my brothers died. I had loved him deeply. He was cultured and unconventional in my traditional and conventional family. He was the one to first read to me "The Prophet" by Gibran Khalil Gibran, and he used to recount to me a long story, that upon growing up I discovered was the legendary myth of "Gilgamesh." I cried bitterly when I heard of his death. But when I saw his face lying in a wooden coffin, my tears stopped for I saw him smiling in deep sleep. I knew then that death is only a transformation, not a tragic ending, that death is part of the formation of the circle of life that is perpetually going on like the day that follows the night ... I left the wake at home. Life was pulsating in the streets outside ...

"During childhood I began to draw and to dream of making statues. In our city there were neither museums nor art schools ... the dream was mysterious ... I would drown in the observation of nature, the formations of earth and rock, the roundness of the hills, their interacting movements. Nature was a human body. ...I borrowed art and literary books from a public library and I started reading Eliot . . . and poetry was another space for freedom and the voyage to the unknown became food for the soul and the spirit....

"By then, I had made my decision and chosen the world of art. For me this was close to a religious commitment - a declaration of faith. The world of art is beautiful and mysterious, in it vision is crystallized and becomes poems, paintings and statues. A fertile, generous world where the seen and the unseen unify ...

"I finished my high school studies in Amman ... I used to read a lot and discuss a lot, especially in religious and existential matters. I felt Amman was small and confined and I had a great urge to know the world ... I carried my drawings, and unknown to my father I left for Beirut - Lebanon where my eldest brother lived

...I told him of my ambitions and what I want of my life ..."

Mona stayed in Beirut for a while. In the early sixties Beirut was a thriving haven for Arab intellectuals, artists and writers who laid the foundations for Arab modernity. She learned a great deal from her encounters and friendships with her contemporary peers. Despite the inspirational climate of Beirut, Mona's real destination was Paris, and with the financial and moral support of her brother she left on a ship to France. Few months later she participated in a contest for admission to the Ecole Nationale Superior des Beaux Arts in Paris. She rated fourth amongst five hundred contestants and Mona was finally a full fledged student of sculpture.

" ... Here I am in Paris, the Paris that I have dreamed of and read about .... In Paris one finds the whole world ... In its museums, art treasures that I used to see in books are in front of me now. I could see them, touch them, and I could talk to them. At the Louvre, I discovered the greatness of our part of the world. The Sumerian and Nabatean sculptures. How I loved the head sculpture of King Gudea, the architect of the land of Sumer and its governor. The Egyptian statues of colored, smoothed granite, the Assyrian hall of the winged bulls, the statue of Nike of Samothrace, the winged Greek goddess of victory, the Blackstone of Moab, whereon King Joshua inscribed the history of his country. I gloried in all these and many other creations that formed milestones in the cultural heritage of man.

" ... I started work at The Ecole des Beaux Arts ... and I studied the formation of the human body which embodies all the elements of creation ... I discovered that the human nudity in art is from the nudity of the earth ... and that the earth is the body, and the body is the earth. Although I came from a traditional and conservative society, I was not surprised by all this, but realized how the body in our country is surrounded with taboos.

"In 1965 ... I created my first sculpture in stone and called it "The Motherhood of the Earth." I had a mysterious feeling that I was finding my own style in sculpture: the reduction of form, its roundness, the form that moves from a central point and extends towards the peripheries, the abstraction of human form, leading

4

to a symbolic presence. From this early work, all my other stone creations were born... My teachers encouraged this approach from the beginning, and found in my style a dedication to the true elements of Arabic art.

"... In 1967 I travelled to Italy where I spent several months being apprenticed to the industrial craftsmen of the marble quarries of Carrara. I returned to Paris in 1968 where I lived the events of "the student revolution". They were important events that opened for me avenues of intellectual and political awareness, of the role of art and its relationship to society and government, the domination of the West over the third world, and many ideas on the freedom of thought and social change. At the end of these events I felt a keen urge to return home, for I knew then that I did not belong to the French society and that the country that I identified with needed me to share in its development. I wanted to become part of the dynamics of Arab social interaction, and help in laying the foundation of modern Arab art, for I came to realize that the West is not superior to the East, neither culturally nor creatively! .... In 1968 I returned to Amman, but soon felt the limitations of the artistic and intellectual life in Jordan at that time, and I realized that I needed more experience and know- how so as to be an effective artist in such an environment.. So I left once again for Beirut, still the undisputed cultural and intellectual capital of the Arab world. I lived there until 1982. "

In the aftermath of the 1982 Israeli invasion of Lebanon, Mona returned to Amman with her daughter Dia. It was a turning point in her personal life and artistic career. She left her home in Beirut as well as her sculptures and memories to seek a peaceful haven, amongst her family. Shattered and grieved by the war, yet full of determination, Mona slowly became an active participant in the life of her home-town. On a cold morning in March of 1984 Mona Saudi's first granite sculpture "Growth" was installed in a prominent location in Amman. She was overjoyed to see her creation become part of the lives of her people. Her work in Jordan progressed with showings, special commissions and a constant flow of both local and foreign visitors who came to see her and admire her sculptures housed in her home "museum."

In 1985 Mona held a solo exhibition at the Alef Gallery in Washington. The following year, the director of the Institut du Monde Arab in Paris expressed a wish to have one of her sculptures at the entrance to its prominent building in Paris. Inspired by the Nabatean statues, Mona created a three meter marble sculpture, "Formations of the Spirit," which was offered as a special gift from Jordan to the Institut.

Though by now an internationally recognized artist, Mona continued her aesthetic searching.

"Sculpture for me is a search in form, and the possibilities of creation are endless. Each time I work, I feel more that I am still at the beginning, and that I have done nothing yet, and when I view all the sculptures that I have chiseled, and that I have intimately known from the moment of their conception in my workshop, I feel a longing to create more and more of these forms. I love to see my work go to museums, to public places and to be owned by all."

All along as Mona expressed herself in the medium of stone, she also explored in the realm of language. She enjoyed writing poetry and her poems went hand in hand with her sculpture. She used them both to express her artistic vision and the yearnings of her soul.

Reading the poetry of Mona Saudi one experiences a tender explosion of the senses, a powerful liberation of emotion. As in her sculptures, Mona's poetry focuses on a few ideas which she pursues to their limits. Frugal in theme and word choice, her smooth lines of poetry create bold and pure imagery that dares to be direct. She is not afraid of omissions. Her poetry is instinctive. Consciously and subconsciously, Mona would knead her hidden yearnings with wisdom and wit. The emotions are controlled and defined. Daring and courageous in the examination of self, the poems are set in a solid structure that follows no particular rhythm, rhyme or scheme, yet the reader senses the presence of a fine craftsman. Mona writes as she sculpts with an attention to detail and a refined sense of language always aiming at purity and abstraction. She is a very private person, intimate with herself, honest to her needs and the demands of her being. She does not succumb to obstacles and faces challenges with an inner strength and a conscious fighting spirit.

For Mona, life is simultaneously complex and simple as black and white - her favorite colors, sophisticated in their proximity and distinctness, carrying in their contradictory shades the intensity of hidden passions and mystical illusions. In her writings and her sculptures, she creatively combines the private with the public.

As I spent the last few months examining her work, and as I studied her words and images, I thought how she must write like she sculpts; wrapped up, intense, captivated, oblivious to all that surrounds her, stone powder all over her face and clothes, enveloped with an expression of tenderness, pain and courage, haunted by a creator's vision searching for meaning and fulfillment. Her sculptures, whether of granite, marble or of humble garden stone, loom strong and powerful over her poems, and in moments of pure magic, poem and sculpture fuse into a glorious tribute to her talents.

Translating Mona's poems was enjoyable and exciting. It was hard and frustrating at times but it was a wonderful creative process throughout which I learned how two different languages, Arabic and English, expressions of two different cultures can become one tool to convey feelings and dreams that carry within them universal values that lie at the depth of human vision and experience.

My translation of Mona Saudi's poetry was an enriching labor of friendship, of love for poetry and the flight of the soul. I hope that they will be a source of inspiration for readers in English as they have been for those who have read them in Arabic.

Tania Tamari Nasir
June 5, 1996

7

1   Departure

I left my home to its walls
And I opened myself a path to the wind

I depart
I become what submerges the sea with prayers and
    grief.

Am I a dream?

The earth is silent
Deserted is the sky
O death, when shall I be?

Paris 1964

2   Circles

The sea tells me we are born and we die.
Like seasons we return
Between light and darkness we move in a circle,
And the circle is in a lamp.

One day, they say, the leaf shall fall.

Paris 1964

3   Return

I know I have lived over a thousand years
And I am yet to be born

4   The Wandering Stranger

I

And how do I enter the silence of stone?
Like the evening enters the city
Wherever I walk, the world opens its arms to the wan-
    dering stranger.

And how do I destroy myself?

Myself: forms of chaos floating between light and dark-
    ness, unified in an image that resembles
god, descending in circles of dust that turn into ashes
    and tears.
Myself: crystal vessels celebrating the union of death
    and despair.

O you wandering stone,
O you wandering stranger,
Tell me, where is my image?

II

. . . "Because as it was said, this wandering stranger
    was an illusion drawn upon invisible paths, he
thought he was in reality, yet in reality, he never knew
    what he was.

A voyage of the unknown was the wandering stranger,
    he was seen everywhere yet was invisible,
and he saw, and became all that he saw: the sea, the
    wind, the sun, the living face and the face of
the dead. "

Paris 1965

الغريب المسافر

- ١ -

كيف أدخل في صمت الحجر : كما يدخل المساءُ
لمدينة
العالم حيث أمشي يفتح ذراعيه ويصممتُ للغريب
المسافر
كيف أسحقُ ذاتي ؟
ذاتي : أشكالُ الفوضى تسبحُ بين النور والعتمة ،
نتوحدُ في شكل كأنّه الله ، ثم تهبطُ في لولب ،
تصيرُ دوائرَ الهباء ،
ماداً بكاء .
ذاتي ، مراكب بلّور في أعراس الموت واليأس ،

أيها الحجر المسافر قُل لي ، أيّها التائه المسافر :
أين شكلي ؟

- ٢ -

لأنه فيما يُقال أنّ الغريبَ المسافرَ كان وهماً مرسوماً
فوق الطرق اللامرئية ، وحسبَ أنّه في الحقيقة ،
في الحقيقة لمْ يدر يوماً ما هو .
كان سَفَرَ المجهول يُرى في كلّ مكان ولا يُرى ،
وكان يُرى ويصيرُ كلّ ما يُرى ،
لبحر ، الريح ، الشمس ، الوجه الحيّ ،
والوجه الميت .

باريس ١٩٦٥

5   Chaos

And how did I come to love you, O earth
Am I invisible, or both of us are
Who sees us?

The city is blind and my vision multiplies in paths of the
      void,
In the chaos of the elements
In the labyrinth of awakening
In the languor of time and the sea
In the languor of the night
Gray pavements are my refuge,
When life suddenly appears carried by the sun.

And how, O ye presence in forgetfulness
I come into the world,
I am the wind, the path and god
Then how should I tell
I listen to the banging of the light in the wind
I descend into the world of miracles through alleys of
      dreams,
Through alleys of the world,
As if I am the truth, moving between form and form-
      lessness
Between the arrival of a season and its departure
Between the vision and its shadow.

Paris 1966

6   Words

I have fallen in love with heaven and earth and with
     what is between heaven and earth . (Words run)
. . . And God was in the roses, the roses were in the
     garden, and the garden was in the city, the
city was in spring, and when the spring was no more in
     the city, the city was no more in the
garden, the garden was no more in the roses, the roses
     were no more in god, there became for
each thing its image and for each I, its own self and for
     each he, his own self.

Melodies circle amongst the stars, the stars circle in my
     head, the night is knotted on the forehead
of the city, the sky embraces the stars, the stars don
     the clouds, the clouds stare into the earth,
as it was said in our time, as it is said in ages gone past
     and ages to come.

Paris 1966

7   A World of Strangeness

He enters a world of strangeness
He mingles with the stars,
His way is drawn upon the air

If I were despair,
If I were the return
Wandering has no end

I saw and I dreamt of cities with no frontiers,
I saw eternal skies, birds that migrate, mountains, men
    and women pulling the carts of day towards
the night, and the carts of night towards the day.
And I saw them move over the illusion of roads and the
    illusion of time,
I saw mountains that dream, and valleys that swim in
    the light, I saw rocks, blue and red, and with
each step the world became stranger still, lines and
    angles expanding.
I saw the chaos of the world become its order and I saw
    the unity of form in changes and contrasts,
I saw the amalgam of opposites, and the union of move-
    ment and constancy.

I saw life and death as one,
And I cried: how glorious, how glorious!

Paris 1967

8   Water

Where do your feet lead you?
The road was a stone,
The trees were green lights
I questioned my footsteps;
I found I am a vessel, and water is the road.

Paris 1967

9 The Black Statue

I found these words in an empty bottle
I do not know their story nor from where they came.
The bottle was on the door of a house, the house was
    suspended above the edge of a street, the
street dangled under a lantern, the lantern was a speck
    that lit the night.

The night was a black statue carved in water and in air.
The estranged self said: could consciousness be re-
    gained
The statue had eyes that see,
I walked over his feet, I entered his labyrinth, and then...
The bottle broke
I gathered the words and climbed the statue
I planted the words in his hands
I put my hands in my pocket
And in ecstasy I entered my kingdom.

Paris 1967

التمثال الأسود

هذه الكلمات وجدتها في زجاجة فارغة ، لا أعرفُ
تاريخها ولا من أين أتت ، كانت الزجاجة على باب
بيت ، وكان البيتُ معلّقاً على طرف طريق ، والطريقُ
معلقة تحت سراج ، والسراجُ ثقب يضيءُ الليل .

كان الليلُ تمثالاً أسودَ منحوتاً في الماء والهواء . .
- (ينبغي أن يعود الوعيُ) ، قالت الذاتُ الغائبة
كان للتمثال عيون الحضور ، مشيتُ فوق قدميه
دخلتُ في دهاليزه ، ثم . . . . .
نكسرت الزجاجة
جمعتُ الكلمات في كفّيّ وصعدتُ فوق درب التمثال ،
زرعتُ الكلمات في يديه ،
وضعتُ يديّ في جيبي ،
ودخلتُ فرحاً في مملكتي .

باريس ١٩٦٧

17

10   Endless Motion

In what city was I born
In what time
From whose womb did I come?

I entered the void -
Presence is absence
Absence is a center
The history of the world has vanished.

What have you seen over the waters?
I saw endless motion.

Paris 1968

11   Stones

I

O estranged stone, ramble alone
No one shall know you
Nor by yourself you shall be recognized
For you have known everything.

II

As if the stones are wandering upon the earth
As if the stones are the soul of the earth
Come forth O god of stone
You, voice of the earth.

III

And then the stones grow and I dissolve,
And when I vanish, the stones declare my birth.

Farewell!

Paris 1968

This Night

And I shall engrave this night upon oblivion
Let the stones sleep
Let them conceive a statue
I hear the rain beating roof tops
The cold wind carrying resounding bells
Let the stones sleep....

Paris 1968

13 Eternity

In the night of stars,
I saw engraved upon the skies of the earth:
The city roaming across the river
The river piercing the heart of the world
The seas roaring between the poles.

I saw the trees, as erected sculptures,
The wall was an eye
The night was an eye
The star was an eye
And the stone was an eye.

In the night of stars,
I saw engraved upon the skies of the earth:
What a traveler over the water sees
What a traveler in the air sees
I saw the eternity of the visible.

Paris 1968

14   A Picture Without a Frame

In the darkness of exile, a horse comes covered with
    dust..
Sleep is a well that does not slumber
The horse advances alone in an open night
It comes out from a picture without a frame
The picture is the whole night
An endless void,
Where the question hangs upon the forehead of time....

Stains of blood on a poster
A bullet
Red blood spreads over the face of the horse and on its
    body
It spots the night
The horse covered with dust remains standing,
And comes forward as if in a picture.....

The woman said: the time of fulfillment has come, in her
    womb a green branch has grown, it
became a tree, that brought forth an apple, her body
    became round, where the whole world sat,
space and God, the stars and all living things.
On the seventh day the moon was born,
She placed it on a platter and offered it to the universe.

Paris 1972

15   Blue Freedom

Now, in the rising of the first moon towards blue free-
   dom
In places that have no name except longing
Woman is the first creation,
A woman with no name, many arms has she and
   mighty like Shiva
She does not injure,
For she is lunar in vision and of the earth in flesh.
Thus she intersects with plants, freedom and with
   dreams,

And where is the point from which nothing begins.

1973

16   Black Paper

Tell me of black paper
Upon which I shall write the history of stones and their
    dreams.
Would that our hearts reveal their secrets?

Will we touch life, and the dream is our way since the
    beginning of time,
when we deserted our homeland and followed the
    dream
And from stones we made friends and gods.

If you should become silent O stone,
And if you abstain,
What shall we say
Should we die
O friends come with me to green loneliness.

Will words of love rise in stones
Will the stone be a movement for silence
And how can we unite love and stone
Words that can be said and words of stillness
And O beloved, how can I be yours and be free
And how can I find you, not to dwell in you
But to awaken you, and for you to awaken me.

1973

الورق الأسود

أخْبِروني عن ورق أسودَ
كتبَ عليه تاريخ الحجارة وأحلامها ،
لو يحكي القلبُ خباياهُ ...
هل نلمسُ الحياةَ والحلمُ طريقُنا من أول
لبدء ، حين هَجَرْنا الوطنَ ورحلنا إليه ،
صارَ لنا من الحجارة أصدقاءٌ وآلهةٌ ..
فإن تصمتي أو تمتنعي يا حجارةً ،
ماذا نقول ؟
نموتُ ؟
يا أصدقاء ، رافقوني في الوحدة الخضراء .

. . .

هل كلامُ الحبِّ يصعدُ في الحجر
يكونُ الحجرُ حركةً للصمت ،
كيف نجمعُ بين الحبِّ والحجر ،
بين كلام يُقال وكلام لا يُقال
يا حبيبي ، كيف أكونُ لكَ وأكونُ دونكَ
ألاقيكَ ، لا لأسكنَ إليكَ
لكن لأوقظكَ وتوقظني !

بيروت ١٩٧٣

25

17   Slow Down O Wings

Slow down o wings
These are the waters of the earth, you are a sun O bird,
And it is motion in the soul,
It cannot be touched
I cannot be touched
We cannot be touched.

We move towards the tangents of the earth
And tremble at its edges
We are charmed by death
We surrender, and for a moment we die.

And how do you endure this whiteness?
Slow down O wings
O green fields, would our hearts become stars, and this
    lover of the earth how could he survive. Who would
    teach me the secrets of the universe. Who would
    connect me with the mystery of men, so that I can
    knead them with my heart, to touch the essence and
    live only by love?.

O glorious light, be my guide and let not darkness in-
    vade my vision.

O waters bless the sadness of my lover, kiss his eyes
    before sleep and before awakening as I used to do,
    and may I not become darkness in his heart, and
    may he not become darkness in mine.

Do not let the walls of illusion grow within us,
Take them O waters, to the deep seas, and transform
them into crystal vessels, children might see them as
stars, and throw them with pebbles

Slow down O wings.

Beirut 1973

18   Women of the Earth

Darkness is a green field,
In the memory of its vision, the fire of genesis dwells
Love and the pulse of stones abide in the dream of our
    deeds
Our first waters.

And take my dream, O women of the earth,
Plant it in your wombs,
Do not be afraid of the night nor be enslaved by the day,

Abide in the page and in the stone, as upon the earth.

Beirut 1974

يا نساء الأرض

لِظلامُ أرضٌ خضراءُ ، في ذاكرة رؤاها نارُ الخليقةِ
لأولى ، ويسكنُ الحبَّ وقلبَ الحجرِ ،
حلُمُ الفعلِ
ماؤُنا الأوَّلَ .

. . . .

يخذْنَ يا نساءَ الأرضِ حلُمي ، ابذرْنَهُ في
أرحامكنَّ ، ولا تخفْنَ الليلَ ولا يأسرْكُنَّ
النهارُ ،
واسكُنَّ في الصفحةِ وفي الحَجَرِ كما على
الأرضِ .

بيروت ١٩٧٤

29

19 The Haunted

Haunted by an embrace or a circle, by the triangle
    sometimes
Haunted by greenness, the scent of earth and rain
    sometimes
Haunted by stones and silence
Possessed by the flesh
This radiant presence that touches death and pen-
    etrates the void
Possessed by fullness, embracing the heart and the
    hand.

From forgetfulness we write the past
For Birth is awaited, yet it is always present..

And lost are our horizons, O bird.

Beirut 1974

20   The Green Stone

This woman was born today in a green stone
From the mountains of Jordan it might have come,
This woman does not know, if her name is rose, cloud
    or stone.

Beirut 1974

21   Despair

Let her die
She who knows not except the path of dreams and the
    womb
Let her die and may nothing be born after her.
O despair untie my hair cover me with roses
I weep in your hands,
I die in your hands, and I smell the earth's fragrance
And I say farewell to dreams of pregnant stone.
They have killed you, they have killed me
And the children shall come with me.

Remember us, O waters!

Beirut 1974

22   Sculptures

And I shall sculpt for you two lovers, always two:
Male - female, mother - earth, son - flesh
Form embracing form, dialogue - silence
And what is in a dream - is upon the earth

Man is the fruit of his dream.

Beirut 1974

تماثيل

«سأنحتُ لكما حبيبين ، دائماً اثنين :
الذكرُ والأنثى ، الأم الأرضُ ، والإبنُ - الجسدُ
«شكلٌ يعانقُ شكلاً ، حوارٌ - صمت . . .

«وما يوجدُ في الحُلُم يوجدُ على الأرض
والإنسانُ نباتُ حُلُمِه .

بيروت ١٩٧٤

33

23   Beirut

The earth is locked
The tree has no door
The sky is a deserted stable

It is written this city is a wall
Chatter floats around the flab of its stomach and its
     thighs
Lifeless words that do not resemble death.
Deep is the stillness.

If only the darkness would open up its living blackness
If only the circle of the sun and the curve of the moon
     would let me reside between them,
Then I would become estranged in an language that
     does connect
In paths that do not reach.

O glorious decline
I offer you my heart
I offer you my deeds

Beirut 1974

I

I begin with my death, and say it is the way
I begin with the call that summons me to creation and
    fertility
I begin with extracting delusion from my eyes
I begin with extracting delusion from yours.

II

And you would say: love was a source that we have not
    known
Intimacy was a field whereon we did not allow the
    dream to grow, the dream which unifies the one with
    the other,
the dream which does not put asunder,
 (Ah, why is it that whenever I come to you, you break
    me?)

Is this how my death is going to be:
I come to you, I find you, and you refrain,
I remain drawn to you and you do not reach me,
My hands stretch out in the vastness of solitude,
And solitude becomes a question of nothingness.

Can I negate love? I die if I negate love, nothing re-
    mains, neither body nor meaning. And how shall I
    face the stones, and how shall I meet the dream, and
    how shall I receive the morning and the night?

(Why do you call me, O death)

Should I not desert you,
(And each time I come to you, you break me)
And each time I go away from you, I return, as if it is
    only you that harvests and plants and dreams, as if
    it is only you who grows in the immensity of the
    heart.
(You might not realize love, until it becomes death)

Let my image desert me

III

My intent was to disperse the solitude and to let flow
    the waters
To recreate the will and to weave the body with love,
Your body and mine, the body of the rose, the grass and
    the leaves,
The body of the earth and the days,
And life becomes a lake of bewilderment.

My intent was to negate death, to let creation flow
That joy should prevail, that the pillars of the earth
    should tremble, not to fall but to float
You cocoon yourself, while I untangle the ropes,
You enter the shell, I go into the crystal
You enter the night, I go into the light.
We become opposites in whiteness,
My call of longing, you turn to silence,
I unburden you from veils and the days, you put on
    illusions.

O star of the moon,
When will the time of your dawning come in the radiant
  voyage?
The purity of my being is a fusion of love and the ele-
  ments
You conceal my spring and its waters.
Forget me, not that I should die, but that I should be
  born
Desert me O images and O dreams forget me,
Why does the path become narrow and lonely
Estrangement is not a home, nor love is an illusion.
And I do not find you!

IV

I say time is short, no confusion in the memory
The night has no shores and the city is a slum
I come to you, I wipe away the illusion
I open a path for a white awakening and I erase all
  memories.

I let fall the walls, yours and mine. I wipe out insomnia
  from the night, and I give myself to another voyage, I
  change my pivot, and I say, you shall come when the
  time comes, and if you do not come, your absence
  will be a new coming, and when I long for you, I shall
  embrace the yearning and I shall love everything
  that towards it grows.

I learn not to build graves, but roam in vastness.

V

I rise in a black stone and learn the secrets of silence
The whiteness of dreams surrounds me
I elude despair, I weave death with my dreams
And I ask the days of the past to bless you
I free the circle and I throw its circumference in the sea.

A dream of passion is woman
A voyage of longing is the earth.

Beirut 1975

25   A Verse

Our dreams are transparent boats
 Where we have dwelt since childhood
 We gave wood to the merchants
 And we chose the waters.

No owners and nothing to be owned.
And we chose the waters.

Beirut 1975

Woman-earth-lover
 It is war-time, blood ignites in the night of the world.
The night is the expansion of an awakening that sur-
    prised the dreamer.

Who is killed?

Loneliness is your blood.
You who have gone, where is your living death,
 So that we can celebrate the splendors of your wed-
    ding?
 And who shall sprinkle a little water on this sunset?

The night of loneliness is coming
In lands that have no roots,
And in places where the soul cannot abide.

Sing O child, so that we can hear
A tender voice in the burning earth
How can they forbid us to dream
When with the dream, our hands are kneaded.

Talk in the language of love, for my heart is aflame!

Beirut 1975

27 Women in a Refugee Camp

Three mothers sat in the courtyard of a house,
Dreaming of a homeland
Talking of sons that have gone or are martyrs,
They remember their country in the passage of time
And they mix the dream with bread and the news.

They question, are they really dead?

The plant was of blue waters
And it was the body of remembrance.

Beirut 1975

The One Who Did Not Depart

To Ghassan Kanafani*

They saw him on the horizon
The evening was a horse orbiting the sun
The sun was the forehead of his dream
And the trees were all longing.

They saw him on the horizon
Whiteness was the waiting of the earth
And his earth was a line of blood.

They saw him on the horizon
Moving in stillness
Steadfast as the storm.

They saw him on the horizon
The horizon was a bird carrying epistles from martyrs,
    to those who shall follow.

They saw him on the horizon
 Dusk was his blood, with it he taught us how to draw:
Faces, mirrors and children.

Beirut 1978

* A Palestinian novelist, assassinated by the Israeli
    Mossad, in Beirut, Lebanon 1972

الذي لم يرحل

الى غسان كنفاني

شاهدوه في الأفق ، وكان المساءُ فرساً
يتمحورُ حول الشمس ،
وكانت الشمسُ جبين حُلمه
والأشجارُ كلّها حنينْ . .

شاهدوه في الأفق وكان البياضُ
انتظارَ الأرض
وأرضه خيطُ دم يجري طريّاً . .

شاهدوه في الأفق ، وكان يتحركُ كأنه
لثبوت ، ويثبت مثل العصف . . .

شاهدوه في الأفق ، وكانَ الأفق طائراً
يحملُ رسائلَ من الشهداءِ إلى مَن
سيستشهدون . .

شاهدوه في الأفق ، وكانَ الشفقُ دمَهُ
ليوميٌّ ، علّمنا أن نرسمَ به وجوهاً
ومرايا ، وأطفالا . .

بيروت ١٩٧٨

29   Childhood

To my daughter Dia*

We stand amidst two wars
A long war that does not end
And another that is coming.

The house is brick tiled,
The tree is in bloom
Dia is learning her first things,
The first sound
The first touch
The first step
She waters me with sudden tranquillity.

Like an oasis in the desert is the face of Dia asleep,
And when she awakes, she takes me to the spring.

Let us rest in childhood
Before we are taken by the coming war.

Beirut 1979

* Dia in Arabic means light.

30   Whiteness

Speech resembling silence
Stone resembling speech
Waiting is a circle and the triangle a path
The square is reality, the rectangle a tomb
The dream is a plant on the edge of a line.

He said: write, draw, walk in whiteness
Look ahead and forget what is behind,
And you shall not arrive...

Beirut 1979

The Earth

To Mahmoud Darwish*

O earth you who were our mother
Your children have nothing to offer anymore
You have become a memory
You are not a past
You are not a future
You are a present scored with wounds,
Like the line of the horizon at dusk
When the sunset freezes
It does not move towards the night,
It does not move towards light.

O Mother, you whom we swear not to forget
Here we are, turning you into an absence
We melt into what does not reach you.

The wound is a horizon at sunset
The night does not come, nor does the light.

And when you ask: does the earth die?
You erase the question lest you commit a sin.

Beirut 1979

* A renowned Palestinian poet.

الأرض

الى محمود درويش

أيتُها الأرضُ التي كنتِ أُمَّنا ،
لم يعُدْ لأبنائك عطاءٌ يمنحونَه ،
ما أنتِ تصيرينَ ذكرى ،
ولستِ ماضياً ولستِ مستقبلاً . . .

إنَّك حاضرٌ مخطَّطٌ بالجروح
كخَطِّ الأفق وقت الشفق ،
والغروبُ كأنَّه يتجمَّدُ ، لا يذهبُ نحو
الليلِ ، لا يذهبُ نحو الضوء . .

أيتُها الأمُّ ، التي نقسمُ ألّا ننساك
ما نحنُ نغتابُكِ ونغيّبُكِ ، ونغيبُ فيما لا يأتي
نحوكِ . . .

والجرحُ خيطُ أفقٍ وقتَ الغروب
لا يأتي الليلُ ، ولا يأتي الضوءُ . . .

وحين تسألُ : هل تموتُ الأرضُ ؟
نمحو السؤالَ لئلا تقع في الخطيئة !

بيروت ١٩٧٩

47

32   Birth

To my daughter Dia

Here is the dream, installed upon the throne of the sky,
    it tears away your shroud so that death
shall not clothe you, and barriers shall not stop you.

You were born as a growing space, you befriended the
    trees and the awakening, the stone and the
waters, the time between the beginning of darkness
    and the beginning of dawn, you never sat on a
chair, nor waited for a sign.

You walked towards a beginning that blossomed, and
    you live in the moment of transformation.
Your days a weaving of light, embracing place and time.
    You do not wait for yourself nor for
another....

Childhood comes to you in "Dia". She tells you of the
    time of buried consciousness, when you were
a sperm, she ties the end of the circle with the begin-
    ning of the primal horizon that rose on the
forehead of man. She tells you, you have not mistaken
    the path of a dream, she points with the
finger of childhood to show you your beginning and
    your end, and says she is your way, and you
are hers; for she has seen all of you, and made you see
    what she beheld.
Your light comes from within, and takes on your forms
She was a revelation for you and you were a revelation
    for her.

Be calm, so that the vision shall erupt as a volcano
    melting the body and the soul.
And you know you can possess all that cannot be pos-
    sessed, that you are the traveler in the womb
of the earth, you who can conceive all births, you who
    are able to forget your forefathers and your
children

And you are the fear in tranquillity.....

Beirut 1980

33   Friends

A strange sadness comes to us at the beginning of
    night,
It breeds on our feet and between our toes,
On the edge of lips and between our teeth
And we fear it will submerge us to death,
So we open windows from which no longing comes
And which do not look upon a homeland.

Today, at the beginning of night, a transparent sadness
    descends:
Friends have become echoes.

Beirut 1980

34   Action

Slow down O speech so we can learn silence,
Assassins are more numerous than bullets,
Slow down O speech;
That we may learn action

Beirut 1981

35   A Walk

I went down to the market this morning
Without combing my hair
Without putting on my shoes
I went down to shout in the silence of the city
To feel the earth under my feet.

I saw the streets empty,
A pink morning illuminates the walls of stone.
I shouted: is any mortal there, is there anyone?
The morning laughed and said: the people are asleep
And if they die, they might wake up.

I am possessed with wonder
The stone is a radiant presence
People are the absence.

Amman 1985

36   A Lullaby

Sleep O Stone, for the night is long
Sleep O stone, for the night is long
And I'll dream of you yet again

Do you remember when for me you were the source of
    fertility
I would take you in my hands, to begin our lovely dia-
    logue
You would be formed amidst the ring of the chisel and
    the bang of the soul.
The living form would be born, in the living act, in the
    living dream.

I long to take you again in my hands
Sleep O stone, for the night is long.

Amman 1987

37   Cantata

To Adonis*

You who are possessed with light
And around you all this darkness
You approach, time and place are a container for your
    dreams
Yours is the steadfastness of stone
The music of the wind and the flowing waters.

In your hands you take a fragment of nothingness
And you form the Creation,
You mix the stone with light
You infuse the dream into the earth
You transform trees into hymns
You wake up every morning as if you were born every
    day
To love the earth and all it holds
And it gives you its offerings
You erase the dust that veils your vision
You polish the days, turning them into pulsating forms
You weave time in the folds of the stone
And curved lines take their course in the expansion of
    the soul
The elements combine in a radiance that only the secret
    of creation can reveal.

And from where should we begin, how?
You who control the flames
Though all you know is how to ignite the fires.

And from where do you capture all this joy
You who are possessed with light?
Yet darkness is all around you!

Amman 1989

* A renowned Syrian poet.

نشيد

إلى أدونيس

أنتَ المأخوذُ بالضَّوءِ ،
وحولك كلُّ هذا الظلامِ ،
تتقدّمُ ، الزمنُ والمكانُ وعاءٌ لأحلامِكَ ،
لكَ ثبوتُ الحجرِ ، وموسيقى الريح
وجريانُ الماءِ

تأخذُ بين يديكَ بعضاً من شيءٍ ، وتصنعُ التكوينَ ،
تُدخلُ الضوءَ في الحجرِ ، تمزجُ الحُلمَ بالأرضِ ،
تحوّلُ الشجرَ إلى نشيد ،
تصحو كلَّ صباحٍ وكأنَّكَ تولدُ كلَّ يومٍ ،
لتعشقَ الأرضَ وما عليها ، وتُعطيكَ عطاياها ،
تمحو كلَّ غَبشٍ يمرُّ أمام عينيكَ ،
تصقُلُ الأيامَ ، تصنعُها أشكالاً تنبضُ ،
تُدخلُ الزمنَ في ثنايا الحجرِ ،
فيأخذُ الخطُّ المنحني مجراه في امتدادات الروحِ ،
وتختلطُ العناصرُ في بهاءٍ لا يعرفُ إلاّ سرُّ الخلقِ .

من أين نبدأ ، كيف ؟
تسيطرُ على الاشتعالاتِ ولا تعرفُ إلاّ أن تُقيمَ الحرائقَ ...

ومن أين يأتيكَ كلُّ هذا الفرحِ ،
أنت المأخوذُ بالضوءِ وحولك كلّ هذا الظلامِ !

عمان ١٩٨٩

55

38   Interventions

I said: let me plough my land so that the rains might fall
And lightning might set the night ablaze.

I said: let me plant my dreams
And a song might resound in this wasteland
I said: let me take a stone
And engrave the wisdom of the days.

He said: the rains will not come
The water will not flow
And madness is your wisdom.

+   +   +

When I found that the city has no heart
I moved to its limbs
I set a black stone at my door to always remember:

   Darkness is but a stepping-stone for light.

Amman 1990

O night of wisdom
O night of silence and of prophecies
O night of the moon.

One dome of sky for the whole earth
One dome of sky for wretchedness and for joy
One dome of sky for remembrance and oblivion.

O magic of this radiant night
O trees carry me upon your wings
So that I may read joy from the book of the earth
And fill time with what is needed to ripen the dream.

And loneliness shall not break me, nor rust conceal.

Amman 1992

To stones from which we build an ocean of dreams
To stones where beginnings and endings abide
To stones pregnant with the longing of revelation

To stones from which I weave the light of joy
To stones in which I chisel a path for the soul
To stones that I touch, and the vapors of love arise
And as I polish them my soul thins out
And the gods of mystery talk to me.

To stones which have taught me the radiance of labor
To stones which I lean on each time
I am touched by fatigue and despair knocks upon my
    door.

To stones which connect me with what I know
And with what I do not know.

I have learnt incarnation to penetrate the unknown,
And I have dwelt between the orbits of labor and the
    orbits of dreams.

Amman 1992

محيط الحلم

حجارةٍ نرفعُ منها محيطَ الحُلم
حجارةٍ تسكنُ فيها بداياتٌ ونهايات
حجارةٍ حبلى بشوق التجليّ

حجارةٍ انسجُ منها ضوءَ الفرح
حجارةٍ انقشُ فيها مسرى الروح
حجارةٍ ألمسها فيتصاعد بخارُ العشق
وأصقلُها فترقُ روحي وتكلّمُني آلهةُ الخفايا

حجارةٍ علّمتني بهاءَ الفعل
حجارةٍ استندُ عليها كلّما مسّني التعبُ أو طرق
بابي اليأسُ . . .
حجارةٍ تصلني بما أعرفُ وبما لا أعرف :

تعلمتُ التجسيدَ لأدخل في الغيب
وسكنتُ بين مداراتِ الحلم ومداراتِ الفعل .

عمان ١٩٩٢

59

41   Moments

At this holy hour
The light sits on the throne of the earth
 Soon it will rise to depart in steps of wisdom
Leaving the night to fill the void.

The toils of the day close their doors
A work begun and another not yet started
And many other things postponed.

The summer sky is naked
Like time before the beginning of time
The birds return to their trees
A mysterious visitor says, "Farewell"

Amman 1993

42   "The Idiot Wind" *

To Mohammed Khalil **

I am possessed by the idiot wind
The storm of black formations
It penetrates the soul
It is revealed in a white square
Where the hand of man touches the dawn of the gods
   in the vastness amongst sparkling galaxies.

It is nothing but a drawing on paper this idiot wind
   whose music I hear flowing in my blood.

Come, not so that I caress you,
But so that I can bathe in your kindness
To wipe the dust which encircles me,
And bring me back to the primal source.

Amman 1993

* A song by Bob Dylan
** An American artist originally from the Sudan.

43   The Mystery Is in the Creation

I had forgotten the fall of light on the body
Remember me, O God
I had forgotten God
Come O goddess of forgetfulness
Plant me as a seed in the earth so that my births con-
    tinue,
And here is death at the edge of the horizon it stands,
Stretching out its arms:
Desire amidst desolate skies.

I had forgotten joy
Would someone knock at my door...
Before I am gathered by the night of doom.

When like me you are alone
Kneaded with prophecies and dreams
Do not touch my body, rise in my soul
So that I shall know your face and your destinations
For it is you that I love
And it is you that I call.

The mystery is in the creation
Shape a vessel in space
Write with the fire of transformation
And do not gather your ashes
Leave them to the wind to take on its way
For they are from the embodiment of the soul
And they hold the pulse of your return.

Be calm, and open your eyes
So that with the light of wonder you touch ecstasy
As death on the edge of the horizon stands
Before it enters the cells and the embryos.

It is the right of the earth our mother, to quake and
    crack
To become a bed for destruction.

It is the right of the wind to uproot trees and all living
    things
To burst into windows and doors by day and by night

It is the right of clouds to carry bolts of lightning
For nature to be violent

But you O Man: do not shoot one single bullet in space.

Amman 1994